Snap books® Babysitter's Backpack

No RUNNING in the HOUSE

Safety Tips Every BABYSITTER Needs to Know

by Rebecca Rissman

Consultant:
Lyn Horning
Assistant Director, Better Kid Care
Penn State University
University Park, Pennsylvania

CAPSTONE PRESS
a capstone imprint

Snap Books are published by Capstone Press,
1710 Roe Crest Drive, North Mankato, Minnesota 56003
www.capstonepub.com

Library of Congress Cataloging-in-Publication Data
Rissman, Rebecca, author.
  No running in the house : safety tips every babysitter needs to know / by Rebecca
Rissman.
      pages cm. — (Babysitter's backpack)
  Summary: "Discusses basic safety precautions and procedures every babysitter needs to
know"—Provided by publisher.
  Audience: Grades 4 to 6.
  Includes index.
ISBN 978-1-4914-0765-3 (library binding)
ISBN 978-1-4914-0769-1 (eBook pdf)
1. Babysitting—Juvenile literature. 2. Safety education—Juvenile literature. 3. Children's
accidents—Prevention—Juvenile literature. I. Title.
  HQ769.5.R57 2015
  649.10248--dc23
                              2014012070

Editorial Credits
Abby Colich, editor; Juliette Peters, designer; Tracy Cummins, media researcher;
Laura Manthe, production specialist

Photo Credits
Capstone Press/Karon Dubke: 2 Right, 3 Left, 4, 8, 9, 10, 11, 12, 13 Top, 14, 16, 17 Top, 19,
24, 25, 27 Top; Getty Images/Fuse: 26; Photoshot/©Caro: 2 Left, 7 Top; Science Source/
Voisin/Phanie: 3 Right, 23 Top; Shutterstock/Denis Cristo: 5 Bottom, 7 Bottom, 13 Bottom,
17 Bottom, 21 Bottom, 23 Bottom, 27 Bottom, 28, Cover, Doungtawan, 15 Inset, Ersler
Dmitry, 20, hugolacasse, Design Element, Mila Supinskaya, 22, Monkey Business Images,
6, 18, Natykach Nataliia, Design Element, Shooarts, 15, Veerachai Viteeman, Design
Element; SuperStock/Voisin/Phanie: 5 Top; Thinkstock/Jupiterimages: 21 Top

Printed in the United States of America in North Mankato, Minnesota
032014   008087CGF14

Table of Contents

CHAPTER 1

Babysitting Basics

Can you name a babysitter's most important job? Is it keeping the house clean or making sure the kids have a good time? That's only part of the job. A babysitter's most important job is keeping the children and herself safe.

To become the safest babysitter on the block, you'll need to enroll in safety training courses. In these classes you'll learn how to avoid dangerous situations and how to stay safe during many common babysitting activities.

What Should You Do quiz questions throughout will help you know if you're ready to be a great babysitter. You can look up the answers on page 28.

What Should You Do?

You only have one week to prepare for your first babysitting job. You should spend that time ...

A learning the basics of child care and safety.
B collecting art supplies for crafts.
C learning a new recipe to cook for the children.
D deciding what to do with your first paycheck.

Before You Begin

Maybe you're interested in earning some extra money, or you watch your younger siblings while your parents aren't home. Before you start babysitting, ask a parent or trusted adult to help you enroll in safety courses. A great place to start is at your local community center or Red Cross. The Red Cross also has several online courses. Youth clubs such as Girl Scouts, Boy Scouts, or 4-H may also offer classes.

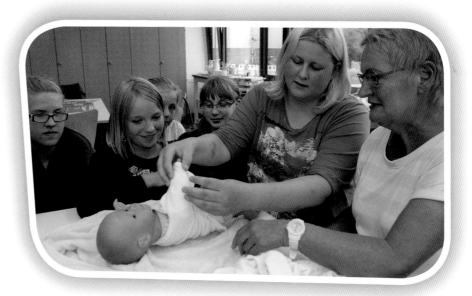

The first class you should take is a basic first aid course. This class will teach you basic first-aid skills. These include how to help someone who is choking or how to properly care for a cut or bruise. You will learn when to call for emergency help and when to handle things yourself. In some classes you may learn how to provide CPR (cardiopulmonary resuscitation) in case a child becomes unconscious and stops breathing.

You should also take a general babysitter training course. You'll learn basic child care such as how to change a diaper and how to properly hold an infant.

What Should You Do?

You are babysitting a toddler who begins vomiting. You should ...

A make the child a bowl of chicken noodle soup.

B call the parents and tell them. Keep the child calm and offer him or her a small drink of water. Clean up the vomit. Then wash your hands.

C ignore it. The parents can take care of it when they get home.

D put the child in bed and clean up the vomit.

CHAPTER 2

Getting Started

How can you be a safe babysitter before you've even accepted your first babysitting job? It's easy! Only accept jobs that you feel prepared to handle safely.

Getting to Know Each Other

Before you babysit for a new family, you should schedule an interview. In this short meeting, you can ask questions and get to know the family. Ask about the ages and number of children they want you to care for. It's also a chance for you to decide if you can safely care for the children. During the interview be sure you find out if:

- you'll be cooking any meals or bathing the children
- any of the children have special medical or physical needs
- you need to give any medications to children
- there is anything else you need to know to keep children safe

If any of the family's answers make you feel uncomfortable or overwhelmed, politely turn down the job.

Caring for Children with Physical or Medical Needs

Some children have special physical or medical needs. Before babysitting for a new family, ask the parents if their children have any conditions you should know about. You should be aware of any illnesses, allergies, or disabilities.

Remember, you're not a doctor. You don't need to know how to do everything. If a child requires medicine or special help, ask the parents to show you what to do. The ability to handle small medical issues is important. When parents know you're prepared, they'll feel more comfortable leaving their children in your care.

Allergy Alert!

Some children have allergies. Their bodies react in a negative way when they come in contact with something they are allergic to. Some children have minor allergies that cause a runny nose, itchy eyes, or a skin rash. Other children have serious allergic reactions that could lead to death. If parents tell you their child has an allergy, be sure to ask these questions:

- What is your child allergic to?
- How do I know if your child is having an allergic reaction?
- What should I do if your child has an allergic reaction?

Always Be Prepared

Make sure you arrive at each babysitting job a few minutes early. The extra time will give you a chance to go over some important information with the parents. Before parents leave, be sure you can answer all of these questions:

- Where are the parents going?
- When will the parents be home?
- At what phone number can the parents be reached?
- Who should you call in case of emergency? What is the phone number or where is it written down?
- What is the address of the home where you are babysitting?
- Are the children having any issues you should know about?

Parents may have written down this information before you arrive. If not be sure you have recorded it in a safe place. Having this information will help you in case of an emergency.

What Should You Do?

You are babysitting a child who is playing a card game. Your friend texts you to ask what you are doing. You should ...

A continue to play the game while texting your friend back. You can multitask!

B go into another room and call her to talk.

C text her back your weekend plans. The child is playing a safe game.

D ignore her texts. You will respond to her later.

Time for a Tour!

When you arrive at a new babysitting job, ask the parents for a home tour. Ask them to show you how to lock the doors and windows and where the fire extinguishers are located. If you will be cooking, ask the parents to show you around the kitchen. If you need to give the children medications, have the parents write down instructions. Make sure you know where the medications are kept. Ask the parents to show you where their home phone is and how to use it.

If the children are allowed outdoors, ask parents if they have any special rules or areas the children should stay within. If the children go to a neighborhood park, ask the parents to write out clear directions. If the home has an alarm system, ask the parents to show you how to use it. Finally, make sure you know where the house keys are kept. That way you can lock the doors and take the keys with you if you take the children to a park.

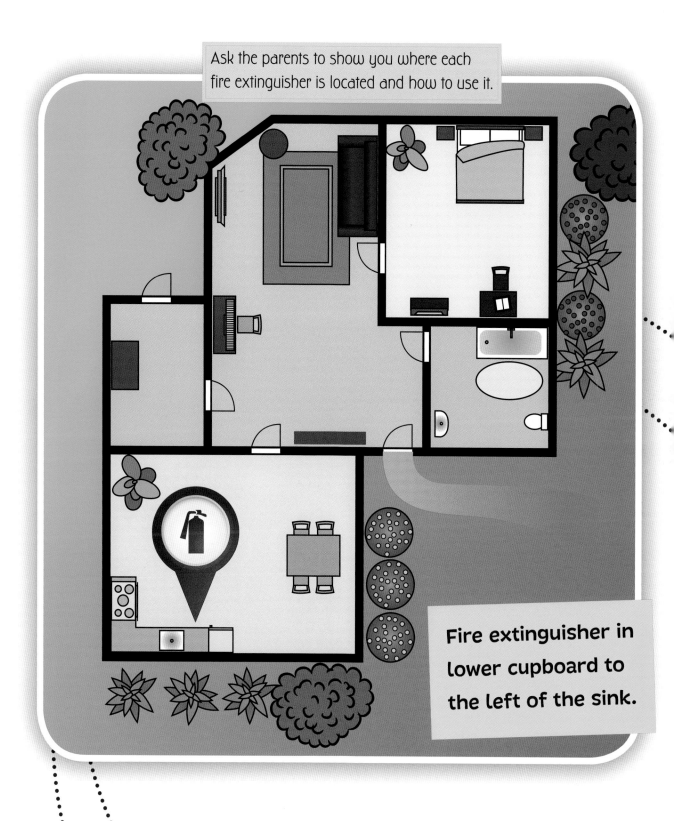

Ask the parents to show you where each fire extinguisher is located and how to use it.

Fire extinguisher in lower cupboard to the left of the sink.

The Number One Rule—Pay Attention!

It might seem like being a safe babysitter is all about following rules and keeping lists. Don't get overwhelmed. There is one rule that will keep you and the kids you're caring for safe—pay attention! Watch the children at all times. Never leave children alone and never let yourself get distracted.

Texting, playing games or checking social media on your phone, or watching TV can be tempting. But good babysitters know that these activities are distracting. Focus your attention on the children you're caring for at all times.

When children are playing, keep them away from unsafe things, including:

- scissors or other sharp objects on a table or shelf
- cords from telephones, window blinds, lamps, or other electrical appliances
- electrical outlets without covers
- small toys or small objects that could be a choking hazard
- breakable dishes or special items on low shelves or tables

Remember, if an accident or emergency happens while you're babysitting, stay calm! Staying calm will help you figure out what action to take.

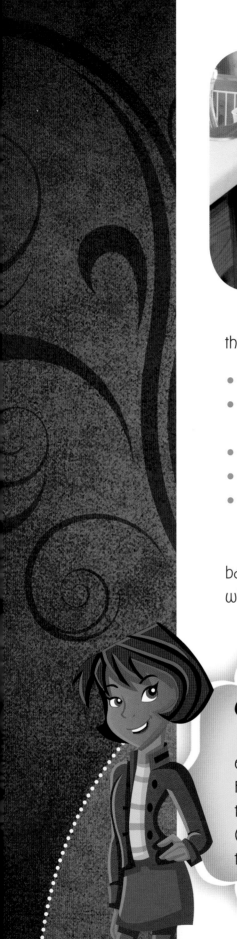

Choking Hazard

Infants and toddlers can easily choke on small objects. For children under 3, that's any toy smaller than 1.75 inches (4.5 centimeters) across. That's the size of this circle.

1¾ inches
4½ centimeters

CHAPTER 4

Always Stay Safe

A babysitter needs to keep safety in mind at all times. Staying safe is easy when you follow safety tips for different activities.

Bath Time

Bath time might seem like a relaxing event for you, but when you're babysitting it's a time to stay on your toes.

> ### Remember!
>
> Children can drown in as little as 1 inch (2.5 cm) of water. Never leave a child alone around any body of water, even if it's shallow.

Babysitters usually don't have to give children a bath. If parents do ask you to bathe their children, be sure to discuss their bath-time routine. Babysitters should never bathe infants.

Before you put a child in the bath, make sure the water isn't too hot. If the children are playing with bath toys, double check that they aren't too small. Young children can choke on small, hard toys. Finally, help children step in and out of the bath. You don't want them to slip and fall.

Pool Safety

What's the best way to spend a hot afternoon? Splashing in the pool, of course! If you are babysitting school-age children, you might take them to a local pool. You must have their parents' permission first. Talk with parents about safety and their children's abilities.

These pool safety tips will keep you and the children safe, happy, and cool:

- Only swim at a pool where a lifeguard is on duty. Never take children swimming in a private backyard pool.
- Don't let children run near the pool.
- Ask the parents what sunscreen or other sun protection children need. Children may need help applying sunscreen.
- Never leave the children alone at a pool—even for a minute!

It is not safe for babysitters to take infants, toddlers, or preschool age children to a swimming pool, even if a lifeguard is present. Younger children can safely cool off on a hot day by splashing around with small amounts of water. Try taking a shallow pan of water and plastic cups outside. Choose a shady area, and join the children as they splash and play.

What Should You Do?

The children you are babysitting want to go swimming, but the parents did not give you permission. You should ...

A politely tell the children that they can go to the pool another time. Suggest a different activity.

B ask all the children if they can swim. If they say yes, take them to the pool.

C call the parents and ask them for permission.

D call a friend and ask if she can help you watch the children at the pool.

Staying Safe While Playing Outdoors

Feeling cooped up indoors? It might be the right time to get outside and enjoy the sunshine. Just remember these safety tips.

- If parents have given you permission to go outdoors, take all the children outside together. Never let one or two children stay inside alone. If one child needs to go inside to use the bathroom, take all the children inside with you. Only go to play areas or parks that the parents told you about. Be sure you know how to get to the play areas so you don't get lost.

- Before going outside, remind children that you must be able to see them at all times. If you walk to a nearby park, the children must hold your hand until you arrive.

- Look around the play area to make sure it's safe. Keep children away from broken glass, pieces of metal, or other sharp objects.

- Playground equipment that is designed for older children is not safe for infants and toddlers. If playground equipment is available for very young children, use the safety straps.

- Do not allow children to play in or near a street or parking lot. If children want to roller skate, rollerblade, bike, or skateboard, make sure they wear helmets and pads. Only play in a car-free area.

Safety Straps

Always fasten the safety straps when you put a young child in a high chair, on a changing table, or in a stroller. Ask the parents if you are unsure of how to properly fasten safety straps. Always stay nearby when a child is strapped into something. Never leave a baby on a bed, sofa, or other raised area.

Staying Safe Around Strangers

You might think the only people you need to worry about while you babysit are the children. Think again. You also need to be very careful around strangers.

If you leave the house, remind children never to go anywhere with strangers or take anything from strangers. Also, never let children use public restrooms by themselves. Always go with them, and take all of the children into the restroom with you.

Even indoors you might still have to deal with strangers. Before the parents leave, ask them if they want you to answer the door or phone while they are gone. If they do, make sure to stay safe. If a stranger comes to the door, never let him or her inside. Tell the stranger the parents are busy and cannot come to the door. Never tell strangers that you are babysitting or that the parents are away. This rule applies to strangers who call on the phone too.

If you ever feel unsafe while you are babysitting, call your parents, a trusted adult, or the police.

Be a Safe Chef!

Some parents might ask you to prepare a meal for the children you are babysitting. Whether this involves the oven, microwave, or no cooking at all, you still need to stay safe. Remember these safety tips so that you don't have to swap your chef's hat for a doctor's coat!

- Get exact information about what to make from the parents and what appliances to use.
- Wash your hands before and after meal preparation.
- Keep children away from sharp tools such as knives or scissors.
- Make sure children don't touch any hot pans or cooking surfaces. When cooking on a stove, turn the handles of pans to the back of the stove.
- Cut food for younger children into very small bites. Sit at a table with the children as they eat. Encourage children to chew their food well.
- Double check that all cooking appliances are turned off after the meal.
- Clean up after the meal carefully. Wipe up any spills. Put leftover food in covered containers, and place them in the refrigerator.

Just because you're busy in the kitchen doesn't mean you can stop paying attention to the children. Give children a quiet, safe activity to do. Make sure the children play near you so you can see them. You need to be sure they are staying safe.

Wash Your Hands

When caring for children, remember to help prevent the spread of germs. Wash your hands before preparing a meal. Wash your hands and the children's hands before and after eating. Also wash your hands after diapering, helping a child use the toilet, wiping a runny nose, and whenever hands are dirty. Washing your hands will help keep you and the children from becoming ill.

What Should You Do? Quiz Answers

page 5

A learning the basics of child care and safety.

Take a first aid or babysitting class if you can. Before you babysit, you need to know how to safely care for children. You'll also learn how to act in an emergency.

page 7

B call the parents and tell them. Keep the child calm and offer him or her a small drink of water. Clean up the vomit. Then wash your hands.

Whenever a child you babysit becomes ill, call and tell the parents. They might have special instructions for you to follow. If a child has vomited, clean him up. Then offer him very small sips of water. Stay with him until the parents return home.

page 13

D ignore her texts. You will respond to her later.

Never text or call your friends while you are babysitting. The children you are caring for need your full attention!

page 21

A politely tell the children that they can go to the pool another time. Suggest a different activity.

Only take children swimming (or on other outings) if their parents have clearly given you permission. Make sure to discuss safety rules with their parents too.

Bonus Questions!

Now that you've reviewed some basic babysitting safety tips, it's time to test your knowledge. What would you do in the following situations?

You are asked to cook dinner for three children. One of the kids wants to help you cook. You should ...

A suggest some ways that the child can safely help.

B tell the child to put on an apron. You don't want clothes getting dirty.

C tell the child that sounds great! Check your e-mail while the child does the work.

D have the child go play in another room. You don't want anyone in the way.

A Depending on the child's age, think of ways the child can safely help as you prepare a meal. Toddlers can help set the table and help you wash fruit and vegetables. Older children can pour milk into cups, tear lettuce to make a salad, and take bowls of cold food to the table. Make sure you can see the child while you are busy cooking.

It's bath time. The 4-year-old you're babysitting likes to take baths alone. You should ...

A stand outside the bathroom door while he takes his bath.

B agree. Tell him to shout for you if he needs anything.

C make sure he has enough bath toys. You don't want him to get bored in there all alone.

D tell him that you need to be in the bathroom with him during his bath to make sure he is safe.

D Reassure him that you will turn around when he gets in and out of the bathtub. Never leave a child alone in the bath.

Glossary

allergy (A-luhr-jee)—an extremely high sensitivity to something in the environment such as dust, pollen, perfume, certain foods, or animals

condition (kuhn-DI-shuhn)—a person's state of health

CPR (CPR)—stands for cardiopulmonary resuscitation; CPR is performed on people who are unconscious and not breathing

disability (dis-uh-BI-luh-tee)—something that restricts people in what they can do; usually because of an illness, injury, or condition present at birth

enroll (in-ROLL)—to sign up for school or a class

hazard (HAZ-urd)—something that is dangerous

interview (IN-tur-vyoo)—to ask someone questions to find out more about something

Read More

American Red Cross. *American Red Cross Babysitter's Training Handbook.* Yardley, Penn.: Staywell, 2008.

Babysitting Secrets: Everything You Need to Have a Successful Babysitting Business. San Francisco: Chronicle Books, 2012.

Bondy, Halley. *Don't Sit on the Baby! The Ultimate Guide to Sane, Skilled, and Safe Babysitting.* San Francisco: Zest Books, 2012.

Internet Sites

FactHound offers a safe, fun way to find Internet sites related to this book. All of the sites on FactHound have been researched by our staff.

Here's all you do:

Visit *www.facthound.com*

Type in this code: 9781491407653

Check out projects, games and lots more at
www.capstonekids.com

Index